Chief of Mission Authority as a Model for National Security Integration

Chief of Mission Authority as a Model for National Security Integration

by Christopher J. Lamb and Edward Marks

Institute for National Strategic Studies
Strategic Perspectives, No. 2

Series Editor: Phillip C. Saunders

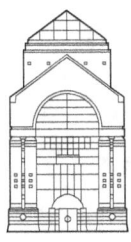

National Defense University Press
Washington, D.C.
December 2010

First printing, December 2010

For current publications of the Institute for National Strategic Studies, please go to the National Defense University Web site at: www.ndu.edu/inss.

Contents

Executive Summary 1

Introduction 3

The Problem 4

A Proximate Solution 12

Implementing the Solution 17

Conclusions 27

Notes 31

Acknowledgments 37

About the Authors 39

Recalling the Goldwater-Nichols legislation of 1986, Secretary Rumsfeld reminded us that to achieve better joint capability, each of the armed services had to "give up some of their turf and authorities and prerogatives." Today, he said, the executive branch is "stove-piped much like the four services were nearly 20 years ago." He wondered if it might be appropriate to ask agencies to "give up some of their existing turf and authority in exchange for a stronger, faster, more efficient government wide joint effort." Privately, other key officials have made the same point to us.

—9/11 Commission Report, 2004

Executive authority below the President is necessary to ensure the effectiveness of contingency relief and reconstruction operations. The role of executive authority—and the lack thereof—over interagency coordination lies at the heart of the failures in the Iraq reconstruction program.

—*Hard Lessons: The Iraq Reconstruction Experience*
Special Inspector General for Iraq Reconstruction, 2009

Executive Summary

The inability of the President of the United States to delegate executive authority for integrating the efforts of departments and agencies on priority missions is a major shortcoming in the way the national security system of the U.S. Government functions. Statutorily assigned missions combined with organizational cultures create "stovepipes" that militate against integrated operations. This obstacle to "unity of effort" has received great attention since 9/11 but continues to adversely affect government operations in an era of increasingly multidisciplinary challenges, from counterproliferation to counterinsurgency in Afghanistan. Presidents have tried various approaches to solving the problem: National Security Council committees, "lead agencies," and "czars," but none have proven effective.

Yet one precedent of a relatively successful cross-agency executive authority does exist: the Chief of Mission authority delegated to U.S. resident Ambassadors. The Congress and White House could build on this precedent to provide the President greater ability to manage complex national security problems while strengthening congressional oversight of such missions. Specifically, this paper makes a case in favor of legislation that gives the President authority to delegate his integration powers to "Mission Managers." Congress would need to provide resources to empower mission accomplishment, and the President would need to ensure that the Mission Manager's authority is used properly and respected by the heads of departments and agencies. This paper argues that while such reform is politically challenging, there are no insuperable legal or organizational obstacles to such reform.

Introduction

The national security system has an authority problem (see figure 1). The problem is high-lighted by the debate over *czars*, Presidential appointees who oversee a particular issue area, often without Senate confirmation.[1] The practice of appointing czars is controversial for the wrong reasons.[2] Commentators worry that czars create confusion and circumvent congressional oversight. What deserves greater attention is why Presidents appoint czars in the first place and what, if anything, should be done about it.[3] When the interagency process fails to produce the cooperation among departments and agencies necessary to solve a national security (or other) problem, Presidents often designate a lead individual—or czar—to do the job because they do not have enough time to do it themselves.

It is widely recognized that the chief executive needs help integrating the diverse departments and agencies, but past attempts to improve interagency cooperation have generally failed because they paid insufficient attention to the difficult problem of authority. New positions or organizations are often created with great fanfare and directed to ensure a coordinated response to some particular national security issue—intelligence, warfighting, reconstruction, or counterterrorism—only to fail because they lack sufficient authority. Ultimately, the departments and agencies in the national security system see little reason to follow their lead.[4]

At the heart of the problem is the inability to reconcile a desire for a clear chain of command from the President down through the heads of the departments and agencies with the need to empower new mechanisms (individuals or organizational constructs) with sufficient authority to integrate efforts across the departments and agencies in pursuit of specified national missions. "Unity of command" from the President on down through the functional departments and agencies seems to preclude "unity of effort" for missions that are intrinsically interagency in nature and cut across those same chains of command.

In this paper, we argue that solving the interagency integration problem requires an expanded Chief of Mission (COM) authority. COM authority is granted to Ambassadors to oversee and direct the activities of employees from diverse government organizations working in a foreign country, but it could also serve as a model for empowering other leaders in the national security system to solve problems requiring interagency cooperation. As we explain, the Chief of Mission model requires expansion to work well beyond the bilateral setting of a U.S. Embassy in a foreign country, including more legal authority, process adjustments, and wider application. However, the model does point a way forward to escape the dilemma that the current system imposes on Presidents who want unity of effort without sacrificing unified command.

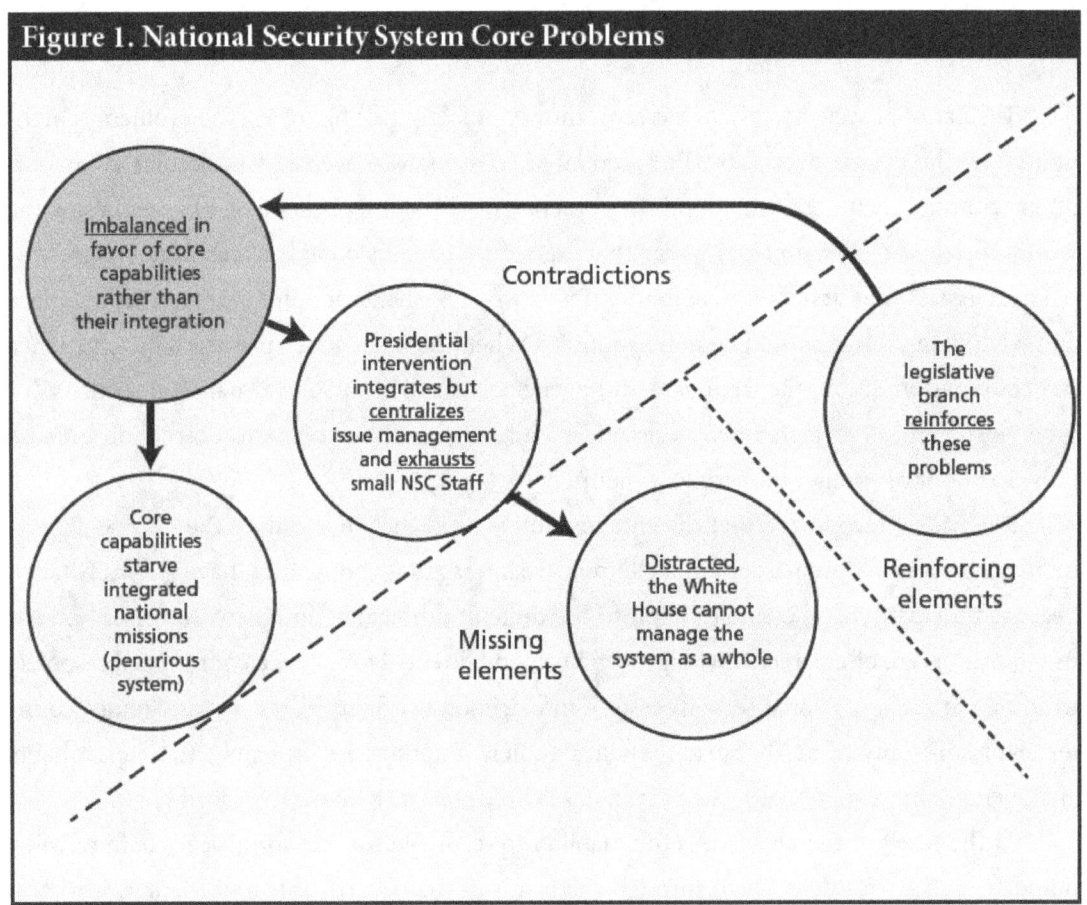

Figure 1. National Security System Core Problems

The Problem

Integrating the work of multiple departments and agencies is an increasingly significant challenge for the modern Presidency because so many problems "cut across a swath of agencies."[5] The need to integrate the activities of the departments and agencies is especially urgent in the realm of national security.[6] Even before the attacks of September 11, 2001, national blue-ribbon panels such as the Hart-Rudman Commission were pointing out the need for better interagency coordination.[7] Since 9/11, prestigious national investigations of the invasions of Afghanistan and Iraq and other priority national security missions have repeatedly found a debilitating lack of interagency cooperation, thus underscoring the persistence of the problem:

> *Everywhere we looked, we found important (and obvious) issues of interagency*
> *coordination that went unattended, sensible Community-wide proposals blocked*
> *by pockets of resistance, and critical disputes left to fester. Strong interagency*

cooperation was more likely to result from bilateral "treaties" between big agencies than from Community-level management. This ground was well-plowed by the 9/11 Commission and by several other important assessments of the Intelligence Community over the past decade.[8]

Many assume the national security advisor and staff should be able to integrate interdepartmental efforts, but there is ample evidence that they cannot do so for multiple reasons,[9] including insufficient authority. The national security advisor is just that—an advisor to the President—and neither the advisor nor staff have any directive authority over the departments and agencies. The problem is more or less acute depending on Presidential management skills, but a persistent and growing liability by all accounts.

Senior leaders with decades of experience working with the National Security Council's hierarchy of interagency committees complain that the system is ineffective, "byzantine," and stultifying.[10] Virtually all scholarly assessments of the national security system similarly conclude that it suffers from inadequate interagency unity of effort.[11] Mere coordination between departments is often a challenge in the national security system, and higher forms of cross-organizational combined effort such as cooperation, collaboration, and integration[12] are progressively rarer. To be clear, in this paper we will be advocating integration, or the executive authority to direct unified effort in pursuit of national objectives. When we use the expression *interagency coordination* it is to depict a lower level of collective effort.

Unity of Command or Unity of Effort?

Impediments to interagency integration are rooted in the basic structure (see figure 2) of the national security system, which is hierarchical and based upon a functional division of labor among powerful departments and agencies with authorities and prerogatives codified in law and often protected by corresponding congressional committees. These departments and agencies resist cooperation with one another.[13] Department heads assert tight control over their subordinates, and strong organizational cultures—reinforced by legislation—create boundaries around departmental activities so that midlevel officials fight off competition from other agencies that might encroach on their "turf." The clear line of authority from the President down through the department and agency heads and their subordinates, often referred to as unity of command, comes at the expense of unity of effort because departments refuse to work together, even on missions of national importance, for fear of losing their powers, prerogatives, and budgets. The President has the authority to direct integrated efforts within congressional statutory

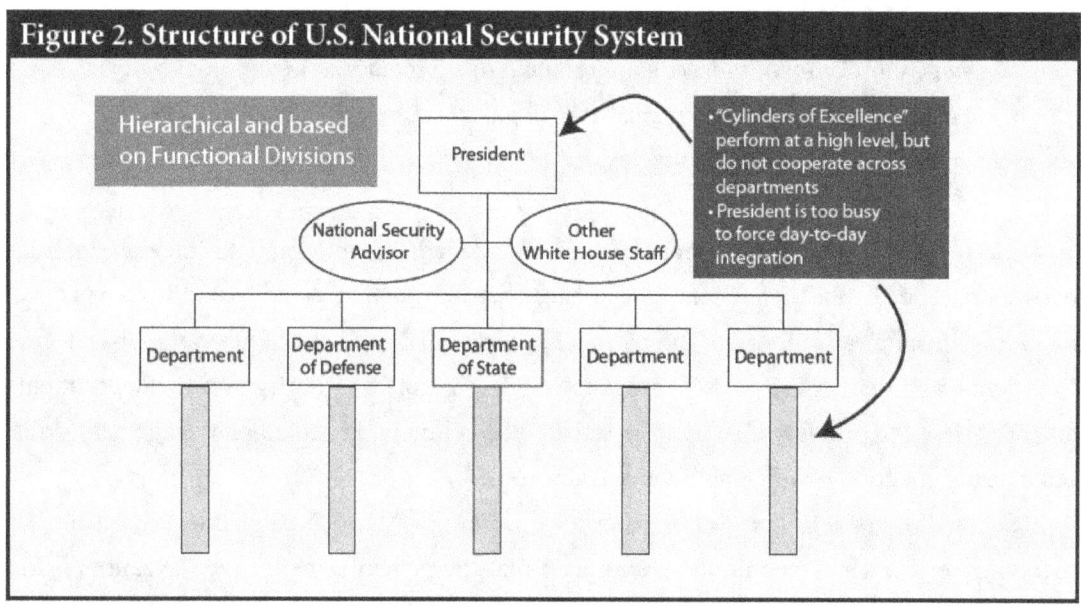

Figure 2. Structure of U.S. National Security System

and financial mandates, so there is little tension between unity of command and effort at the top of the organizational pyramid.

However, this happy circumstance only extends as far as the President's immediate control and attention. The President is too busy to orchestrate cooperation himself except in extraordinary circumstances. Moreover, funding for activities is directed by Congress through the departments and agencies for specific purposes, which further complicates attempts to pursue integrated multiagency efforts. Thus, for most foreign policy matters, the system's basic structure favors vertical departmental lines of authority over horizontal integration across the government.

The system's tendency to favor unity of command (also known as vertical integration), or the principle that any given subordinate should report to only one superior, is an increasingly acute problem because the security environment is increasingly complex and dynamic. The challenges posed by the security environment since the end of World War II require multidisciplinary and thus multiagency responses. The increasing transnational movement of people, knowledge, trade, investments, communications, and cultural identities over the past several decades makes this even truer. A similarly complex and dynamic global business environment has forced many U.S. businesses to balance their organizations with a combination of vertical and horizontal coordination mechanisms. The national security system has not adapted so successfully. Congress as well as Democratic and Republican Presidents have implemented a wide range of reforms to improve the horizontal integration capabilities of the executive branch, but so far, all the mechanisms tried have been found wanting.

Insufficient Reforms and Workarounds

The aforementioned czars are one option that Presidents use to correct the system's tendency to favor vertical rather than horizontal integration. It is often assumed that czars are powerful and that their use will lead to excessive executive power without necessary oversight. In reality, the de jure authority of czars is weak. Most czars have no statutory authority and thus no legal power over other government actors:[14] "That is not to say that members of the White House staff are not and may not be highly influential . . . [but] no executive actor has any obligation to follow the instructions of a member of the White House staff who lacks statutory authority, except insofar as those instructions relay the President's."[15]

When Presidents try to informally delegate their integration authority to a czar, they find the czar's authority is questioned by the departments and agencies. Czars become poor facsimiles of "cajolers-in-chief":

> *Czars, like lead agencies, lack authority to direct Cabinet officials or their organizations. As presidents recognize, czars ". . . will appear to the cabinet secretaries to fuzz up their direct lines to the president." Presidents choose czars hoping they will be able to informally cajole or otherwise orchestrate a higher degree of collaboration, not because they are empowered to compel collaboration. The czar may lower his or her expectations and simply play an honest broker role, but they will still be viewed as interested parties because of their proximity to the president, much the same way Cabinet officials perceive the national security advisor.[16]*

Some czars manage to do good things without having meaningful authority. As the Assistant to the President and Deputy National Security Advisor for Iraq and Afghanistan (the "war czar"), Lieutenant General Douglas Lute, USA, was charged to be the "full-time manager for the implementation and execution of our strategies for Iraq and Afghanistan" but with no control over budgets or personnel.[17] He had to resort to "incessant, relentless pounding and pestering"[18] to improve civilian support for operations in Iraq.[19] Czars can also make headway if the President backs them up consistently, but such persistent Presidential attention is almost as demanding for the President as doing the job directly and tends to defeat the purpose of the czar. Thus, czars are a prominent but not a particularly effective model of Presidentially delegated authority for integration. Presidents use them but recognize their limitations, as do Cabinet officials.[20]

Special Envoys are another type of individual charged with ensuring interagency coordination. Secretary of State Hillary Clinton charged Richard Holbrooke in January 2009 with "coordinat[ing] the entire government effort to achieve United States' strategic goals" in the Afghanistan-Pakistan region.[21] Holbrooke reported directly to the Secretary of State, but he had no statutory authority within the State Department and his position was inherently at odds with that of the Assistant Secretary for South and Central Asia who otherwise conducts oversight of political affairs in Afghanistan and Pakistan. Indeed, Secretary Clinton indirectly acknowledged Holbrooke's poverty of authority when asked whether or not Holbrooke would have direct authority over the Embassies in Kabul and Islamabad: "They'll work through the regular State Department machinery, but in collaboration. . . . I expect everyone to work together. And you know, we're going to be [looking to] Richard to provide . . . leadership."[22]

Another popular integration mechanism is the designation of a "lead agency" to coordinate the efforts of all the departments and agencies involved in solving a complex problem. For example, following the failure of the Coalition Provisional Authority to adequately provide for the reconstruction of Iraq, President George W. Bush ordered the Secretary of State to "coordinate and lead integrated United States Government efforts, involving all U.S. Departments and Agencies with relevant capabilities, to prepare, plan for, and conduct stabilization and reconstruction activities."[23] This order was not accompanied by statutory authority to compel cooperation from other agencies. The Reconstruction and Stabilization Civilian Management Act of 2008 was supposed to clarify and strengthen the role of the Office of the Coordinator for Reconstruction and Stabilization, but it only gives the State Department authority to monitor, plan, and coordinate reconstruction rather than actual operational or budgetary control.[24] Since lead agencies are not properly empowered to integrate effort across the departments and agencies, other organizations often withhold meaningful cooperation. The witticism is true: "lead agency really means sole agency" since other organizations will not follow the lead agency if its directions have a negative impact on their perceived organizational equities.[25]

Joint Interagency Coordination Groups (JIACGs) are another option for improving interagency coordination. Their authority is limited to information-sharing and advisory functions. Originally intended to consist of a mostly civilian staff, JIACGs were designed to equip U.S. military commands to better operate within the interagency community by improving communication.[26] Even this modest objective is difficult, however, as JIACGs are not properly staffed. The relevant departments and agencies largely left the positions unfilled, and they had to be manned by retirees or military personnel. Proponents of JIACGs have argued that their organization and tasks need to be reformed if they are to successfully fulfill even their limited advisory functions.[27]

Similar staffing and authority issues plague the most prominent new interagency organizational construct in the field: Provincial Reconstruction Teams (PRTs). PRTs are interagency groups responsible for rebuilding the infrastructures of Iraq and Afghanistan. A congressional investigation of PRTs did a good job of identifying the inherently weak integration authority given to PRT leaders, which:

> *results in a lack of unity of purpose. Among the efforts at staffing, training, applying lessons learned, and planning, there is no one person or organization in the lead for the "whole of government." When "no further action" is taken, but the mission is not complete, someone must step up to lead. That leader must be empowered to direct the "whole of government" PRT, and larger, stabilization and reconstruction efforts.*[28]

The committee's investigation highlights the system's preference for preserving unity of command for departments and agencies over their personnel on interagency teams such as PRTs. Coordination and planning for PRTs is particularly poor in Washington, DC, where these are conducted independently agency by agency.[29]

Similar limitations plague the performance of other new interagency organizations such as the National Counterterrorism Center and U.S. Africa Command (which is actually a DOD entity with interagency aspirations).[30] The national security system's structural deficiency in interagency coordination is widespread and persistent but not immutable. Other organizations with functional structures balance the need for a clear chain of command with the need for unity of effort across functional divisions of labor (see figure 3). Put differently, organizations must both divide labor to create specialized bodies of expertise (differentiation) and then integrate those bodies of expertise to accomplish missions that require a multidisciplinary effort. Where this balancing act takes place depends on how centralized the organization is. Typically organizations require a mix of centralized efficiencies and decentralized responsiveness; too much centralization creates paralysis and too much decentralization creates chaos.[31]

The "Labor Integration" Problem and Legislative Limitations

The national security system's "labor integration" problem is twofold. First, current practices leave responsibility for integrating the work of multiple departments and agencies far too centralized in the person of the President. At the risk of flippancy, the President is "commander in brief"—his interventions on national security matters are seldom sustained and never

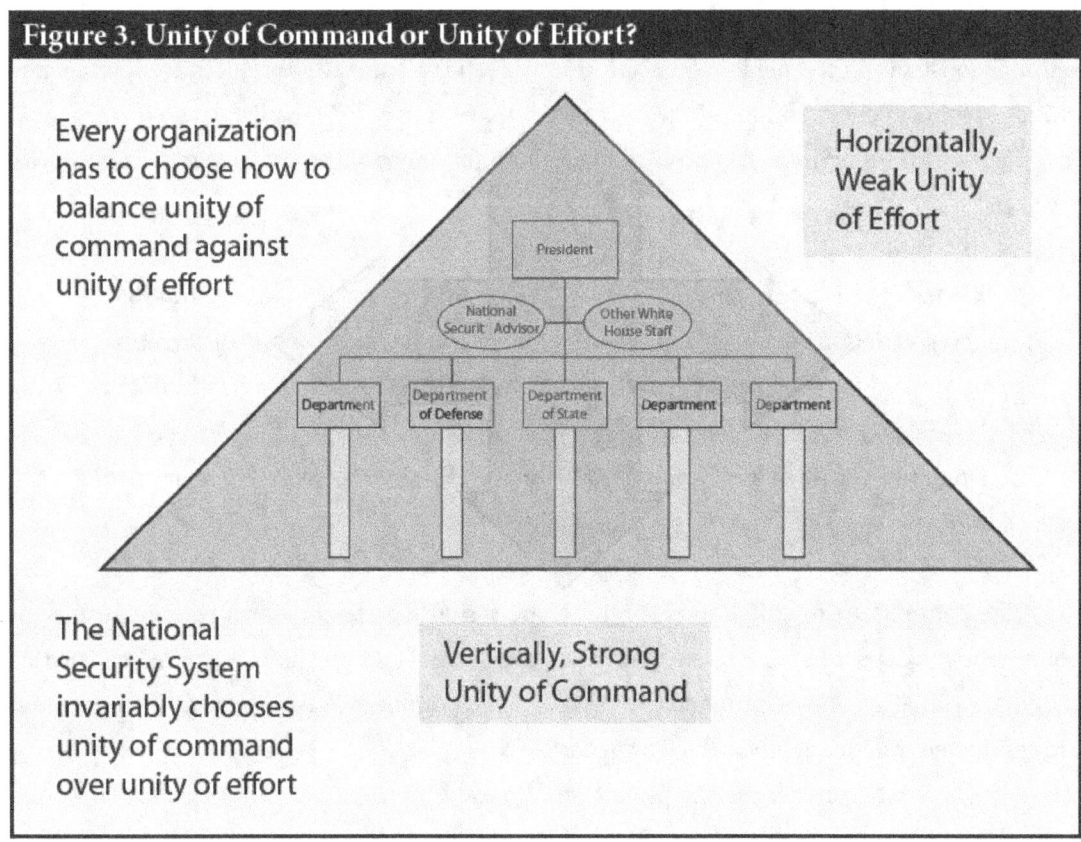

Figure 3. Unity of Command or Unity of Effort?

Every organization has to choose how to balance unity of command against unity of effort

Horizontally, Weak Unity of Effort

President

National Securit Advisor

Other White House Staff

Department

Department of Defense

Department of State

Department

Department

The National Security System invariably chooses unity of command over unity of effort

Vertically, Strong Unity of Command

comprehensive. Modern Presidents with diverse temperaments, experiences, and management styles all find they do not have the time to intervene personally to provide the requisite degree of integration for multidisciplinary national security problems.[32] Thus, challenges are frequently managed through semi-autonomous departments and agencies. In this way, the system defaults to differentiation at the expense of integration, and to unity of command at the expense of unity of effort. In sum, this is what happened when the Department of Defense (DOD) took the lead for postwar planning in Iraq.[33] The problematic tendency to devalue integrated effort becomes much more acute in dynamic and complex environments where multidisciplinary (or intrinsically interagency) problems are the norm.

Second, whenever Congress and the President attempt to strengthen horizontal integration, they end up backing away and substantially curtailing integration powers. Typically, they either skirt the authority issue by creating advisory positions with no real authority for integration, or they provide integration authorities not commensurate with the responsibilities of the position. For example, when Congress decided to create a Weapons of Mass Destruction (WMD) czar,[34] it gave the position substantial responsibilities for formulating interagency plans to counter WMD and terrorism and for leading interagency coordination to deal with them. However, Congress also made clear that the WMD czar was just the *principal advisor to the President* on issues relating to WMD and terrorism, and that even obtaining necessary expertise from the departments and agencies had to be done "with the concurrence of the Secretary of a department or head of an agency."[35]

In the case of the Director of National Intelligence (DNI), Congress provided more authority. The DNI has the authority to "manage and direct the tasking of, collection, analysis, production and dissemination of national intelligence."[36] The DNI was also given budget authority over the Intelligence Community including components of Cabinet-level departments that had intelligence functions. The DNI would not only develop, plan, and direct the budget, but also would have the power to transfer funds between different entities. The DNI could also transfer personnel within the Intelligence Community.[37] At the same time, however, Congress offered the heads of existing departments and agencies an "escape clause," Section 1018, which states:

> *The President shall issue guidelines to ensure the effective implementation and execution within the executive branch of the authorities granted to the Director of National Intelligence by this title and the amendments made by this title, in a manner that respects and does not abrogate the statutory responsibilities of the heads of the departments of the United States Government concerning such departments.*[38]

Section 1018 allows departments and agencies to assert that DNI initiatives impinge on their organization's prerogatives, thus excusing their lack of support. President Bush later attempted to redress the situation in his July 2008 revision of Executive Order 12333, effectively making Cabinet secretaries the *only* executive branch officials who could invoke the charge of abrogation, but the impact of this change is disputed.

Better models of Presidentially delegated integration authority have been used, but they are rare. The example most frequently cited is President Lyndon Johnson's Civil Operations and Rural Development Support (CORDS) program,[39] which was responsible for the implementation of all plans and operations in support of the pacification of Vietnam. Johnson gave the head of CORDS clear authority over both civilian and military personnel.[40] Another example of a more "empowered" interagency integration mechanism might be the Office of National Drug Control Policy (ONDCP), whose director has authority to provide oversight, direction, and coordination for all executive branch departments and agencies involved in combating illegal substances, and importantly also has the responsibility and authority to review and amend their budgets as necessary.[41] This authority is notable yet insufficient.[42] Only one ONDCP director dared to substantially revise departmental budgets, and the ability of the departments to push back was formidable enough that the exercise was not repeated.[43]

Perhaps the best known model of Presidentially delegated authority for integration of diverse department and agency activities, however, is the Chief of Mission authority generally associated with resident bilateral Ambassadors. Its origin, effectiveness, and limitations merit close scrutiny because the model suggests that the national security system's problem with insufficient integration authority will not be solved until Congress provides the President with a legally sanctioned and sufficiently empowered mechanism to integrate the activities of the departments and agencies for priority national missions.

A Proximate Solution

After World War II, the expansion of U.S. programs overseas exacerbated interagency coordination problems. The immediate postwar years saw the establishment of numerous semi-autonomous special missions, the stationing abroad of representatives by many departments and agencies, and the retention of an extensive overseas military establishment: "No clear and enforceable guidance existed to coordinate local U.S. policy in countries such as Greece, where three independent US Missions—Diplomatic, Military, and Economic Aid—pursued their own agendas."[44] By 1948, the authority of the Ambassador had reached a low point with the establishment of largely independent aid missions. In 1949, President Herbert Hoover's Report to President Harry Truman concluded that Ambassadors should have "the ultimate authority overseas with respect to the foreign affairs aspects of program operations."[45]

The first attempt to codify this concept was the Clay Paper, a memorandum of understanding on February 12, 1951, in which the Departments of State and Defense and the Economic Cooperation Administration (predecessor to the U.S. Agency for International Development) established the principle of the Country Team, although not by that name, and made a clear statement of the primary position of the Ambassador.[46] Two months afterward, President Truman wrote to Secretary of State Dean Acheson: "At the country level, all US representatives to that country must speak and act in a consistent manner. The US Ambassador is the representative of the President of the United States to the country and he is responsible for assuring a coordinated US position."[47]

President Dwight Eisenhower began the practice of sending individual letters to every Ambassador tasking them as Chief of Mission "to exercise full responsibility for the direction, coordination, and supervision of all Executive branch US offices and personnel," with three exceptions including "personnel under the command of a US area military commander." Later instructions were sent to all diplomatic posts noting the President's concern that "the representatives of all US agencies in each foreign country are subject to the supervision and leadership of the Chief of Mission," that the Chief of Mission has specific additional responsibilities with respect to mutual security activities, and that in "discharging his responsibilities the Chief of Mission will need and should have the close collaboration of representations of all US agencies."[48]

From 1951 to 1961, the Ambassador's responsibility and authority as Chief of Mission[49] were consolidated by a series of executive orders, Presidential letters and memoranda, and State Department instructions. Early in his administration, President John F. Kennedy reaffirmed this policy in a letter sent to all Ambassadors and department heads. A detailed discussion of this policy, which noted the continuity with key documents issued by the Eisenhower administration, was distributed in a July 8, 1961, memorandum to all Chiefs of Mission entitled "Leadership and Supervisory Responsibility of the Ambassador."[50] As Under Secretary of State for Administration William Crockett wrote on January 25, 1965, in response to a Johnson White House request for background on the role of the Ambassador: "The letter issued by President Kennedy was probably the clearest and strongest affirmation of the doctrine of Ambassador executive authority. Its effect was to elevate the Ambassador from chairman of the Country Team . . . to the man in charge."[51]

Kennedy's instructions were particularly emphatic, but every President since Eisenhower has used the same language as their predecessors when delegating authority to their Chiefs of Mission.

Current Application

Congress codified Chiefs of Mission authority in the Foreign Service Act of 1980 (Public Law 96–465, October 17, 1980) during the Carter administration,[52] which then incorporated the language into the Department of State Foreign Affairs Manual (3 FAM 7112.1). The law states that:

Under the direction of the President, the chief of mission to a foreign country:

(1) shall have full responsibility for the direction, coordination, and supervision of all Government executive branch employees in that country (except for employees under the command of a United States area military commander); and

(2) shall keep fully and currently informed with respect to all activities and operations of the Government within that country, and shall insure that all Government executive branch employees in that country (except for employees under the command of a United States area military commander) comply fully with all applicable directives of the chief of mission.

In exercising these broad responsibilities, Ambassadors can use several tools to obtain compliance from agency players.[53] National Security Decision Directive 38 gives a Chief of Mission control over the "size, composition and mandate of overseas full-time mission staffing for all U.S. Government agencies."[54] In addition, Chiefs of Mission have the power to grant or deny permission to enter their areas of responsibility to any U.S. Government personnel (that is, "country clearance"). Finally, a Chief of Mission can force individuals who are recalcitrant, obstinate, or rebellious to leave their Embassy and the country. These are powerful if seldom used bureaucratic weapons, but there are also other aspects of COM authority that make it a unique contribution to the management of foreign affairs by the U.S. Government.

First, Chief of Mission authority is not a Department of State construct that elevates one department as first among equals. It is true that COM authority is delegated only to resident Ambassadors, that Ambassadors typically are directed to communicate to the President through the Secretary of State,[55] and that some Ambassadors are perceived as too focused on Department of State equities. However, Presidents have long conferred Ambassadorial status and COM authority on political appointees with diverse private and public sector backgrounds, as well as on career Foreign Service Officers. COM authority is in fact an extension of the President's need for personal representation of his powers and authorities to integrate government-wide efforts, and not just an additional authority for the State Department.

Second, Chief of Mission authority is not only an executive branch construct but also an authority sanctioned by Congress in statute. Arguably the same holds true for the Chief of Mission's Country Team concept, which serves as the organizational structure through which COM authority is exercised. Country Teams are a logical extension of COM authority and have been organized and operated to behave more like teams than committees or coalitions of autonomous organizations. The Chief of Mission composes the Country Team from different organizational representatives who serve under his direction and are subject to the Chief of Mission's explicitly delegated Presidential authority for "integrating executive branch activities within his or her geographic domain." There still is no statutory or regulatory basis for its composition and functions. However, when Congress enacted the Mutual Security Act of 1951, it essentially conceived the "Country Team" concept by requiring the President to "assure coordination among representatives of the [U.S. Government] in each country, under the leadership of the Chief of the US Diplomatic Mission." McGeorge Bundy, President Kennedy's National Security Advisor, allegedly coined the term *Country Team* a decade or so later, but Congress formulated the team's mission. Thus, both the Chief of Mission authority and its derivative, the Country Team, are strongly sanctioned by the congressional and executive branches, which means the organizational construct is more likely to endure and be respected.[56]

Third, the continuous use of Chief of Mission authority over multiple decades in hundreds of U.S. Embassies and foreign missions makes it the best established and understood model of interagency decisionmaking. Joint Interagency Task Forces (JIATFs) established to deal with the narcotics problem are a more recent, less prevalent, attempt at creating integrated bureaucratic organizations. Like Country Teams, some JIATFs work better than others. Typically, however, they are empowered with more ambiguous integration authorities. Country Teams led by Chiefs of Mission are the better recognized and empowered model.

Thus, Chief of Mission authority provides the President with the clearest and most forceful cross-departmental executive authority mechanism in use today. The longstanding, well-recognized status of COM authority; the fact that it is agreed upon by both Congress and the President; the link between the authority and the collaborative team decisionmaking model; and the fact that the authority can be conferred on any person of stature with Senate confirmation all bode well for expanding the model for greater use in the national security system. It does, however, have some limitations that must be recognized and corrected.

Limitations

From the beginning, there has been some ambiguity in the interpretation of the extent of the executive authority being delegated. The law confers great responsibility on the Chief of Mission, but section (2) also adds the familiar congressional "limiting clause" with the conditional phrase: "all applicable directives." Other departments and agencies sometimes dispute what constitutes an applicable COM directive, requiring on-the-ground disagreements to be sent up respective chains of command, ultimately to be resolved when necessary by Cabinet-level or Presidential authority. This has been especially true with those departments that also conduct extensive "foreign" operations: U.S. Agency for International Development, DOD, and the Central Intelligence Agency.

In addition, the Chief of Mission authority is provided only to Ambassadors assigned to represent the United States in a specific country. This complicates the Ambassador's relationship with departments and agencies with regional as well as country-specific responsibilities, especially DOD and some intelligence agencies. The Ambassador's relationship with intelligence agencies is complicated by their concern for protecting their sources and methods, the disclosure of which they often claim lies outside the responsibility to the Chief of Mission. Despite persistent confirmation from the highest authorities that intelligence personnel have been "instructed by . . .

headquarters to insure that you [the Ambassador] are sufficiently informed of covert action projects and espionage and clandestine counterintelligence programs to enable you to make an informed judgment as to the political risks involved,"[57] conflicts continue to surface.

With DOD, the relationship is complicated by the separate and somewhat overlapping authority of the regional combatant commanders to control U.S. forces in the field.[58] Also, it can be argued that the DOD "quest for more operational flexibility" against terrorists since 9/11 has eroded COM authority:

> *the Defense Department has championed programs that would allow military operations to be conducted without the explicit concurrence of the COM. The argument has been advanced that there is a compelling security need to be able to conduct operations quickly and the requirement to get COM approval adds an unnecessary level of bureaucratic complexity.*[59]

Conflicts between DOD and Ambassadors are nothing new, but urgent counterterrorism objectives have exacerbated the problem as has the recent dramatic expansion of DOD responsibilities in areas such as postconflict reconstruction.

Given the mixed record, there has been much commentary over the years on the degree to which the combined Chief of Mission and Country Team model has actually been successful in managing interagency integration.[60] Many observers recognize that there is a gap between a Chief of Mission's de jure and de facto authority as the tendency of other agency representatives to independently pursue their organization's equities remains strong. George Kennan once observed that personnel overseas "seem to operate directly or indirectly under the authority of Washington bosses, some in the State Department, some elsewhere." More recently, the Special Inspector General for Iraq Reconstruction commented in his final report that "agency personnel always report to their department heads in Washington," which will "inevitably exert a countervailing force on interagency coordination."[61]

A paper on this subject by Ambassador Robert Oakley and Michael Casey reviewed this question in some detail, arriving at telling insights. Citing the Department of State's Overseas Presence Advisory Panel, Ambassador Oakley noted the core problem with Country Team management was that "Other agencies often view the Ambassador as the Department [of State's] representative, rather than the President's."[62] Because the Ambassador is often perceived as someone pursuing Department of State interests rather than national interests, agencies encourage their personnel on the Country Team to pursue their own objectives and lines of operation, without adequate consultation or coordination. Among other things, Chiefs of Mission lack the proper tools to exert their authority, such as effective control over employee performance reports. There are no built-in incentives for Country Team members, or their parent organizations, to put the priorities of the Country Team above those of individual agencies. In addition, the Presidential letter to Ambassadors does not spell out the specific responsibilities of other agencies vis-à-vis the Ambassador. For these and other reasons, there remains a significant chasm between the Chief of Mission's formal authority and his ability to exercise it.

In short, while the Chief of Mission and Country Team model works well enough most of the time in most Embassies, this is not always the case,[63] and even when it works, there are questions as to whether it should work better.[64] Despite some limitations, the COM model is the best interagency executive authority mechanism available. It does require some enhancement, however, if it is to be put to broader use, which we will refer to from here on as "expanded" COM authority.

Implementing the Solution

Currently, COM authority is limited to the geographic confines of bilateral interstate relations and also allows for major exceptions such as the command of military forces and intelligence operations. It requires modification if it is to be applied more generally and effectively as we recommend. The "mission" in Chief of Mission authority needs to be broadened to include national security problems that exist outside the bilateral authority of a resident Ambassador and intrinsically require multiagency solutions for which no single department or agency has sufficient executive authority and resources. In this model, COM authority is extended for the sole purpose of executing a particular mission, and the authority extends only as far as is required for success. Applying this modification to COM authority would be conceptually, bureaucratically, and legally challenging.

Delimiting Ambassadors' authority has always been a challenge, but at least they could argue that if it occurred in "their" country, then it was their business. Interagency missions unconstrained by a well-defined geographic boundary—for example, eliminating piracy in the world's major oil trading routes—would be more difficult to delimit. The person in charge of executing the mission would have to act on the basis of an approved strategy that balances desired objectives with affordable plans for accomplishing them. Within the scope of this approved strategy, the person (or mission team) afforded expanded COM authority would have to be given presumptive authority to act on behalf of the President to direct departments and agencies to support the implementation of the strategy. Just like the President, the person armed with expanded COM authority would oversee the management of the problem "end to end," from policy and strategy to planning and execution. He or she would tackle and correct any critical impediment preventing mission success, not just establish broad policy and objectives.[65]

Heads of departments and agencies will resist direction from anyone with expanded COM authority. They naturally will be inclined to preserve the unity of command relationship between themselves and the President. While challenging, this tension between vertical unity of command and horizontal unity of effort is a common organizational problem that can and must be managed. The way forward can be depicted as a simple process, presuming Congress has granted the requisite statutory authority and that it is supported with the active involvement of the President, who will be required to ensure his Cabinet officials understand, appreciate, and support the process.

First, the President, with the assistance of the national security advisor, determines that a particularly important issue is an intrinsically interagency problem that requires evoking the congressionally sanctioned and expanded COM authority, which might look something like the following:

> *The President may designate individuals, subject to Senate confirmation, to lead interagency teams to manage clearly defined missions with responsibility for and presumptive authority to direct and coordinate the activities and operations of all of U.S. Government organizations in so far as their support is required to ensure the successful implementation of a Presidentially approved strategy for accomplishing the mission. The designated individual's presumptive authority will not extend beyond the requirements for successful strategy implementation, and department and agency heads may appeal any of the designated individual's decisions to the President if they believe there is a compelling case that executing the decision would do grave harm to other missions of national importance.*

Then, after Senate advice and consent, the individual empowered with expanded COM authority (which we call "the Mission Manager") assembles his team of experts (see figure 4) with the support of the national security staff and begins operations. After investigating the problem and developing alternative strategies to manage or resolve it, assessing associated costs and risks, and obtaining Presidential approval for a particular strategy, the Mission Manager directs its execution. The approved strategy will help the Mission Manager make the case to Congress for resources and help define the limits of the Mission Manager's presumptive authority over diverse department and agency activities.

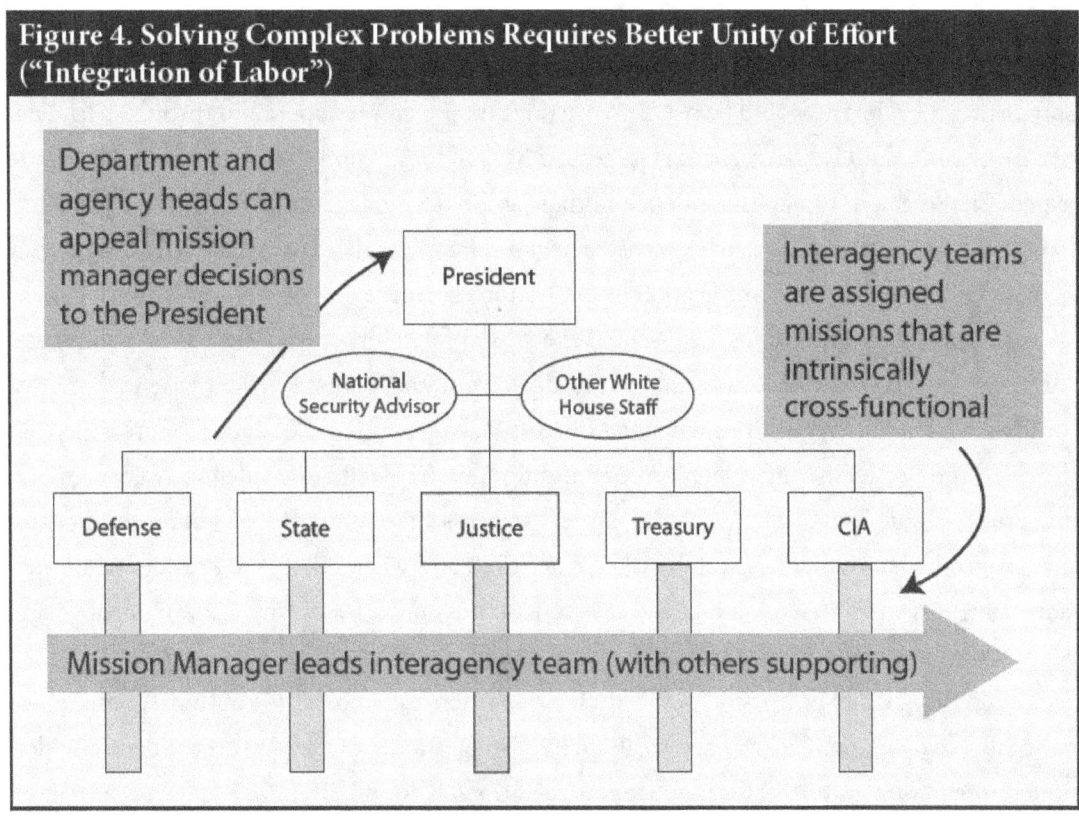

Figure 4. Solving Complex Problems Requires Better Unity of Effort ("Integration of Labor")

In the event that senior functional leaders in the vertical chain of command (that is, the department or agency head) believe a decision by the Mission Manager prevents them from successfully executing their own functional mission, they request a Presidential review. The national security staff then prepares the President for the decision and he makes it. Cabinet officials must be convinced that their equities can be protected from overzealous mission managers. They must retain the right to object when a Mission Manager's pursuit of mission cost too much in terms of its impact on other missions or the long-term sustainability of the core capabilities resident in the national security system's departments and agencies. Similarly, mission managers cannot allow petty organizational equities to repeatedly trump their ability to successfully execute an interagency mission for the President. When department heads and mission managers disagree on the relative risks involved and best way forward, the President should intervene rather than allow such weighty decisions to be made by lesser officials or left to fester. In other words, run correctly, this process should ensure that the President is presented with momentous matters that only he can or should resolve.

The first step in this straightforward process is critically important. The President and Cabinet must be convinced the mission is of national importance and intrinsically interagency so that success is unlikely without a carefully orchestrated effort from multiple agencies. If the mission were deemed largely a military or diplomatic enterprise with other departments simply supporting the effort, it would be better to organize interagency cooperation through a lead department, DOD and Department of State respectively in these examples. Cabinet officials would expect the President to have confidence in their ability to manage missions that are predominantly in their functional area of expertise. However, missions that are intrinsically interagency efforts could be supported for the good of the Nation's security.

This process only outlines the essential executive branch process. It is essential to note that Mission Managers, as all executive branch leaders, would have to make their case to Congress for funding, assisted by the President and Office of Management and Budget. Congress also has provided the President with some limited funding transfer flexibility under the Economy Act and other specific legislation, but by and large, Congress still requires that its appropriation actions control what money is spent, by whom, on what, and when. Thus, the President and Mission Managers would have to make the case to Congress for funding any initiatives above and beyond the expected activities of the departments and agencies.

Modifying Chief of Mission authority to strengthen and expand the authority would also be legally challenging. Preliminary legal analysis suggests the principle of Presidentially delegated integration authority for interagency operations is sound. The President may, pursuant to 3 U.S.C. § 301, delegate particular functions to "the head of any department or agency in the executive branch, or any official thereof" who is subject to Senate confirmation. To qualify as a delegable function, a function must be "vested in the President by law" or vested in another officer who performs the function "subject to the approval, ratification, or other action of the President."[66] These requirements argue for Senate confirmation of Mission Managers, and thus for codifying the expanded COM authorities in law rather than by executive order. In addition, such an important and difficult "good government" reform should be a legislative-executive branch partnership. The reform is much more likely to work as intended if it is sanctioned by Congress and implemented willingly by the President.

Codifying the new authorities in statute is also probably a legal requirement as Gordon Lederman, the former leader of the Project on National Security Reform's Legal Working Group, makes clear.[67] Lederman concludes, "Any individual in the interagency space who exercises meaningful authority to compel departments to act" would have to be an "officer of the United States," and officers of the United States must have their positions established by statute as required by the Appointments Clause of the Constitution. Another reason for codifying the authorities in statute is the need to secure resources for the President's Mission Manager: "The President may create structures and processes and fund them temporarily by transferring resources, but ultimately it is Congress that provides resources on a sustained basis. Without Congress's input and resources, a Presidentially imposed solution to interagency integration may wither for lack of funding."[68] Thus, the statute that modifies COM authority would likely also require a mechanism for funding their activities and associated congressional oversight.

The statute would also have to codify the Mission Managers' presumptive authority over functional activities within the sphere of their mission assignment. Presumptive authority is relatively simple to grasp but would be difficult to codify in law. Congress would have to avoid "escape" clauses for the departments and agencies, instead relying on the President and process to ensure its legitimate concerns are taken into account (that is, that horizontal and vertical integration requirements are balanced by the chief executive). Among other things, the legislative language would have to navigate the issue of civilian control of military forces in crisis environments carefully, as it did in the Goldwater-Nichols reforms that empowered combatant commanders with more horizontal integration authority at the expense of the military services vertical integration authority.

In summary, we advocate an expanded use of the Chief of Mission authority, an expansion that entails both legal and process changes. The authority would be given to individuals and their teams charged with interagency missions of national import, not only to resident Ambassadors. The authority would be limited to the scope of the assigned mission, but not by the de jure authority of department and agency heads. On the contrary, the legislative language would specify that the Mission Manager has presumptive directive authority to manage the problem for the President "end to end," from policy and strategy to planning and execution. Moreover, the Senate would confirm the President's Mission Manager and Congress could also provide resources for the mission. The legislative authority would be administered by process changes involving the President, beginning with the identification of inherently interagency missions of national import, approval of a resource-constrained strategy, and concluding with the President hearing and resolving any challenges to Mission Manager decisions by department heads.

Addressing Objections

Some may object that this model is a radical departure from current practice and too complicated. In fact, this model is simply a more effective and explicit means of balancing competing authorities that draws upon a number of partial precedents. For example, like the Director of National Intelligence, the Mission Manager would be given presumptive authority for horizontal integration (unity of effort) defined not by geographic boundaries but by mission imperatives. Similarly, the right of the senior functional leader in the vertical chain of command (that is, the department or agency head) to dispute a decision by the Mission Manager reflects a process currently in use by various existing mechanisms, such as the interagency Committee on Foreign Investment in the United States. Established executive branch procedure allows the Committee to request a Presidential decision whenever a subject is so contentious that the Committee cannot resolve an issue.[69]

Others may object that the balance between vertical integration (unified chain of command through functional organizations) and horizontal integration (unity of effort across functional organizations) proposed here is either politically naïve or too complicated. One main concern expressed on the political front is that a Cabinet official's diminished authority for complex interagency missions would render his position unattractive. That seems unlikely. Building the world's best military, diplomatic, or intelligence (or other functional) capability and employing those capabilities well when they are assigned lead agency status is still a big and attractive job. Cabinet officials cannot now effectively execute inherently interagency missions, so why would they lament the loss of a responsibility for which they had no practical authority? Military Service chiefs did not turn down opportunities to lead their Services once Congress empowered combatant commanders to lead joint military operations, and it is unlikely that talented people would turn down Cabinet positions because Congress provides the President with an option for employing interagency Mission Managers when circumstances demand such a model.

Thus, the expanded Chief of Mission model would actually facilitate clear roles and missions rather than complicate them. The heads of departments and agencies would ensure national capabilities in their functional areas and oversee and execute missions that require primarily or exclusively their functional expertise (for example, diplomacy, military, or intelligence). The Mission Managers, armed with expanded COM authority, would pursue missions that require tight integration of multiple elements of national power to accomplish a well-defined task. They would take an end-to-end look at complex, multifunctional problems, freeing up senior leaders of functional organizations to focus on problems resident within their domains.

These horizontal leaders and their teams would intervene selectively to eliminate friction and suboptimal efforts where component parts of the organization are not collaborating to maximum effect. They would have presumptive authority to drill down to whatever level of detail is necessary to identify the origin of suboptimal performance and eliminate it. They could use resources made available by Congress specifically for their mission, much the same way Congress and the executive branch (through the National Interdiction Command and Control Plan) require certain counternarcotics funds to be spent through the JIATFs.[70] Alternatively, they could direct specific remedial actions by other organizations that would be legally permissible within existing legislative authorities. The presumption is that the President would back up the Mission Manager's authority to intervene and obtain the desired results.

Some also might object that requiring the President to play traffic cop between horizontal and vertical integrators (that is, leaders for select, priority interagency missions and leaders responsible for ongoing functional capabilities and missions) would be unduly burdensome to the President. Quite the contrary is the case. The leaders of functional organizations would have to accommodate horizontal team decisions or make a direct appeal to the President if they think the Mission Manager has gone too far. However, they would only be inclined to raise the most serious and principled objections. Their dissent could not be based on petty organizational equities or their credibility with the President would diminish. If their concern was a legitimate one, it would be precisely the kind of difficult tradeoff that a President ought to hear and resolve. For example, in 2007 President Bush had to decide whether to support his Iraq "Mission Managers" (General David Petraeus and Ambassador Ryan Crocker) with a troop surge in a bid to reverse a deteriorating situation even though it arguably opened up risk on the Korean Peninsula and undermined the longer term viability of the Army.

Finally, some will argue that skillful use of expanded Chief of Mission authority would be critically dependent upon extremely talented individuals. This is true, but not a liability for the recommendation made here. We are not arguing that talented leaders are unnecessary, but rather that good leaders must be empowered to be more consistently effective. Over the longer term, building a cadre of experienced, multidisciplinary, interagency senior leadership and tracking their careers ought to be a long-term objective for a reformed national security system. In the near term, Presidents would have to choose talented individuals from different backgrounds, including not only senior Ambassadors but also talented generals and even private sector leaders. There are many available. All too often, the system ignores and retires talented, experienced national security leaders too early, and many would jump at the chance to execute priority national missions if they were empowered for success. Moreover, since those empowered with expanded COM authority would have the means to accomplish their objectives, they would be accountable for their performance and could be justifiably replaced for failure to make sufficient progress.[71] This approach would be much more sensible than the current practice of assigning weighty responsibilities without commensurate authorities.

Applying the Expanded Use of COM Authority

One advantage to the expanded Chief of Mission model we advocate is that it could be implemented on a limited basis and then expanded as it proves its worth. Initially, the authority might be made available only to specified executive branch officials for crisis or emergency situations (political or natural) requiring an expeditionary effort by the United States—for example, a tsunami, earthquake, genocide, United Nations peacekeeping operation, or an "Iraq" or "Afghanistan." Many crises we face today, especially natural catastrophes such as the Asian tsunami or the Haitian earthquake, require the mobilization and deployment of a range of U.S. Government capabilities (air and sea transport, medical assistance, emergency supplies, reconstruction assistance) often in coordination with international organizations and other governments. While this sort of challenge is relatively straightforward, it does pose coordination problems. Often, especially with manmade crises, there are political and complicated financial questions, which become more difficult as the first shock is met and transition to reconstruction is pursued. Kosovo and Darfur are excellent examples of manmade problems with serious political implications.

Currently, standard practice is to establish a partnership between the regional combatant commander and the Ambassador on the ground. If there is no resident Ambassador, as in Kosovo, then the partnership is even more ad hoc with someone from Washington drafted into the role. These partnerships can work reasonably well, depending on the scope of the problem and personalities involved, but often in a delayed and hesitant manner as questions of authority, personnel, and funds need to be sorted out from scratch each time, and performance suffers accordingly.

Initially, the expanded Chief of Mission model should be used in crisis or emergency situations, which would be the easiest political and managerial option to implement. The President, acting with congressional authorization, could expand the authority of the resident Ambassador to cover all additional U.S. personnel and resources flowing to the emergency, including military forces. For instance, in the recent Haiti emergency, the American Ambassador in Port-au-Prince could have been immediately designated as the overall relief coordinator for the U.S. Government with expanded COM authority. If it was decided, for any of a number of reasons, that the resident Ambassador would not be the best choice for the job, or if there were no resident Ambassador, then someone else would be appointed.

Congress and the National Security Council staff would have to oversee and manage the crisis teams, which would be small (a leader with 8 to 10 additional team members) and not onerous to assemble. Congress would want progress reports from the Mission Manager, particularly if Congress was providing additional emergency funding as presumably would be the case. National Security Council staff would support the President by making sure the Mission Manager's direction to involved departments and agencies did not exceed the scope of the mission definition or its approved strategy. After the model proves itself and detailed implementation challenges are worked out, use of the expanded COM authority model might be expanded.

The next logical step would be to use the model to cover regional problems of sufficient import to require an interagency empowered executive—for example, the Israeli-Palestinian issue, our multilateral security relations in Afghanistan-Pakistan and surrounding countries, or the containment of North Korean nuclear capabilities. The North Korean nuclear problem is a good example of a likely case for an empowered interagency special envoy to coordinate U.S. policy and operations. Only a careful orchestration of diverse department and agency activities is likely to have any chance of influencing North Korean behavior. Situations such as "Af-Pak" and Darfur and perhaps even the Israeli-Palestinian conflict also may be intrinsically inter-agency problems, requiring more than a purely diplomatic response and representative.

While dramatic crises grab our attention, inadequate coordination within the government dealing with steady-state operations was the original reason for COM authority. A strong case can be made for eventually using COM authority at the headquarters level in the management of steady-state operations. The model could be used to empower the leadership cadres of standing interagency organizations such as the National Counterterrorism Center or joint interagency task forces. Such standing organizations are larger, more resource intensive, and constitute a greater investment by the national security system, but they still require empowered leadership with an interagency team representative similar to Ambassadors and their Country Teams. Over time, the expanded COM model also could be extended to support steady-state management of complex foreign affairs as one of the authors has recently suggested in "The Next Generation Department of State."[72]

However selectively or broadly expanded Chief of Mission authority is applied, it would provide for greater transparency and oversight by Congress as well as the White House. Committees and other bureaucratic "confederations" are notoriously difficult to hold accountable because their authority is not commensurate with their responsibilities. The sharply segmented Federal bureaucracy not only frustrates the President's desire for well-integrated executive branch problem-solving, but it also poses serious oversight problems for Congress as it attempts to find and fix responsibility. Single managers of cross-agency programs, with clear-cut executive responsibility, could more easily be held responsible and more effectively monitored by Congress. Congressional oversight would begin with the enactment of the appropriate amendments to existing statutory authority, be followed by the Senate's advice and consent authority in the appointment of Mission Managers, and where special funding was made available by Congress, would extend to the monitoring of the Mission Manager and team's use of funds by Congress and congressional investigative organizations such as the Government Accountability Office (GAO). Congress would have to decide which of its committees had oversight of particular multiagency

Mission Managers, which would be politically challenging and another reason to begin slowly and apply the authority in crisis situations where the public would demand quick action.

Sufficient authority for interagency leadership is not the only organizational challenge confronting the national security system, but it is a critical one that must eventually be confronted. Research under way at the National Defense University on interagency teams demonstrates that they can be effective without new authorities, operating informally on the basis of voluntary consensus. However, such interagency teams are slow to develop, fragile, and erratic in performance. As one notably successful leader of interagency teams recently lamented, there is still "no effective, consistent mechanism that brings a whole interagency team to focus on a particular foreign policy issue."[73] The absence of such an interagency authority mechanism means that the United States must roll the dice and hope for the best every time it tackles an intrinsically interagency problem. A better solution for interagency missions is required and the solution must involve new authorities.

Past interagency reform efforts in the Clinton and Bush administration put the cart before the horse, trying to improve interagency training and education, assignment procedures, interagency planning, and other processes. Similarly, the current administration promotes the interagency education and staffing efforts made by U.S. Southern Command and U.S. Africa Command, but the GAO found that their laudable initiatives still lacked the "coordination mechanisms . . . critical to achieving integrated approaches."[74] Human capital and process improvements would improve the practical application of expanded COM authority, but the new, empowered interagency executive authority must come first. Once empowered interagency teams exist, the other necessary organizational functions that should support them (education, training, personnel management, planning processes, and so forth) would have a natural focal point for their activities. Currently, such initiatives and activities founder because they are not actually connected to authoritative decision mechanisms. Like the child in the rear seat playing with a toy steering wheel, their efforts are not able to determine direction and drive outcomes.

Once Congress and the President have created empowered interagency authorities, additional steps could be taken to improve interagency performance. For example, as we better understand missions that require interagency participation, it would help for Congress to assign a clear role for different departments and agencies in those mission areas.[75] Before Congress and President Ronald Reagan made it clear in the 1980s that drug interdiction was a matter of national security and that the Department of Defense had a supporting role in that mission, DOD refused to provide meaningful support. If Congress and the President clarify the limited but critical roles of departments and agencies in various national security scenarios, it will be easier for interagency Mission Managers to exercise their presumptive authority to coordinate the diverse departments and agencies that must come together to forge a whole-of-government solution to the problem.

Finally, with the passage of time, the national security system's organizational culture would evolve so that departments and agencies would accept their functional roles and allow interagency Mission Managers to conduct interagency operations. This is what happened in DOD after the Goldwater-Nichols legislation mandated joint military operations. Initially, the military Services fiercely resisted the new combatant commanders who provided horizontal integration across the Services in the conduct of multi-Service combat missions. The Navy, for example, was quick to use its right of appeal to the Secretary of Defense when the decision was made to send Navy special operations forces to U.S. Special Operations Command and Navy ships to U.S. Transportation Command. Both objections were overruled by the Secretary of Defense, of course, and the Navy and other Services were thereafter more reticent to argue narrow parochialism in the face of the department's broader interests.[76] Eventually, the Services embraced their roles as functional authorities (raising, training, and equipping forces for Service-centric missions) and now eagerly support combatant commanders when it comes time to employ joint military forces. If Congress gives the President the authority to delegate his integration powers to a Mission Manager and resources to empower mission accomplishment, and the President ensures these authorities are used and respected by the heads of departments and agencies, the same cultural transformation will occur in the larger national security system.

Conclusions

Virtually all serious observers of national security affairs now recognize that the current structure of the national security system militates against unified problem-solving when the problem is a multiagency issue. The question is what to do about it. In the past the most common reason offered for why difficult interagency reform is unnecessary has been the assertion that good, collaborative leaders can overcome the problem. But history demonstrates such personality-driven successes are the exception rather than the rule.[77] Presidents find that even carefully selected national security "dream teams" consisting of leaders with similar priorities and personal respect for one another end up at odds over difficult issues and taking action that militates against collaboration. The lack of authoritative decisionmaking below the level of the President makes the interagency coordination system so stultifying that it encourages senior leaders to work around the system to get things done, which in practice can mean even less interagency cooperation (see textbox). The 9/11 Commission noted that good leaders can sometimes overcome poor organization but they ought not to have to do so. This sentiment is now widely shared, and as a result interest in interagency reform is at an all-time high.

In fact, the perennial lament that interagency integration is inadequate[78] has turned into a clarion call for reform. One of the latest in an increasingly long line of major national study efforts has reached the conclusion that we need to take a new look at interagency legislation and executive orders undergirding U.S. national security. A report of the independent Quadrennial Defense Review panel led by Stephen Hadley and William Perry finds that the executive branch lacks an effective whole-of-government capacity that integrates the planning and execution capabilities of the many Federal departments and agencies that have national security responsibilities. Among its various recommendations is the need to "[e]stablish standing interagency teams with capabilities to plan for and exercise, in an integrated way, departmental and agency responsibilities in predefined mission scenarios before a crisis occurs."[79]

The recommendation for interagency teams is a good one. But just as Country Teams could not work well without COM authority, interagency teams will not work well without expanded COM authority. One of the most basic rules in good organization is not to assign responsibilities without commensurate authority. Our national security system routinely assigns leaders interagency integration responsibilities without commensurate authority, and the unsatisfactory results repeatedly demonstrate the folly of doing so. As the Government Accountability Office recently recognized, inadequate interagency collaboration results in poorly executed national security missions and also gross inefficiencies that are increasingly onerous and unsustainable.[80] The Special Inspector's report on Iraq, which identified billions of dollars of waste in postconflict reconstruction efforts, similarly concludes: "Executive authority below the President is necessary to ensure the effectiveness of contingency relief and reconstruction operations. The role of executive authority—and the lack thereof—over interagency coordination lies at the heart of the failures in the Iraq reconstruction program."[81] By way of solution the GAO recommends Congress consider creating collaborative organizations with the "resources or authorities . . . needed to further support integrated or mutually supportive activities across agencies."[82]

We agree. The national security system does need stronger executive authority below the level of the President to execute intrinsically interagency missions efficiently and effectively. The expanded COM authority advocated here meets this requirement. It would be difficult to craft and implement, and would require the cooperation of both the legislative and executive branches.[83] However, some improved executive authority for interagency integration below the level of the President and under his supervision is a critical prerequisite for any meaningful interagency reform and for improved national security performance in complex contingencies more gener-

Current System Obstructs Collaborative Leadership

Former Secretary of Defense Donald Rumsfeld was considered both a strong advocate for interagency reform during his tenure and a zealous protector of his department's prerogatives. For example, he notably recommended to the 9/11 Commission that agencies perhaps should "give up some of their existing turf and authority in exchange for a stronger, faster, more efficient government wide joint effort." On the other hand, there are many examples of Secretary Rumsfeld spurning interagency collaboration in practice. For example, one source notes his dissatisfaction when military commanders shared planning with the Department of State:

> *Rumsfeld's problem wasn't with the strategy. He was angry at what he considered a grave bureaucratic sin. [General George] Casey had shared a version of his plan with the U.S. embassy in Baghdad. . . . The ambassador, in turn, had informed the State Department, and somehow Rumsfeld had found out about it. . . . The Defense secretary . . . was an expert bureaucratic infighter who wanted to control the flow of information to the president. He didn't want the State Department to see the plan until it was shown to Bush. By that point, it would be too late for Condoleezza Rice and her aids to muck around with it.*[1]

National Security Council staff confided to one of the authors that the discrepancy between what Secretary Rumsfeld advocated and what he practiced raised more than a few eyebrows at the White House. However, the Secretary could easily have responded to such observations that "you go to war with the national security system you have, not the one you would like to have." In the current system, as Secretary Rumsfeld noted on another occasion, "we end up spending incredible amounts of time that just kind of suck the life out of you at the end of the day spending 4, 5, 6 hours in interagency meetings and the reason is, is because the organization of the government fit the last century instead of this century."[2] In such circumstances, it often seems advisable to go with the strongest department or agency, even when doing so means inadequate interagency collaboration on an intrinsically interagency problem. This explains why the Department of Defense was given the lead for postwar reconstruction in Iraq even when other departments and agencies would necessarily have to be involved.

[1] Greg Jaffe and David Cloud, *The Fourth Star: Four Generals and the Epic Struggle for the Future of the United States Army* (New York: Crown, 2009), 191.

[2] Project on National Security Reform (PNSR) and Center for the Study of the Presidency, *Forging a New Shield* (Arlington, VA: PNSR, 2008), available at <www.pnsr.org/data/files/pnsr_forging_a_new_shield_report.pdf>, 124, 227, fn. 592.

ally. The stakes are high and the critical need for better interagency integration is widely agreed upon. In these circumstances implementing interagency reform can be seen as a litmus test on the ability of the Republic to rise to the demands of its current security environment.

Notes

[1] Usually *czars* are understood to be Presidential appointees who do not have to be confirmed by the Senate, although the term is sometimes extended to cover individuals whose position was created by legislation.

[2] David J. Rothkopf, "It's Official: Obama Creates More Czars than the Romanovs," *Foreign Policy*, April 16, 2009, available at <http://rothkopf.foreignpolicy.com/posts/2009/04/16/its_official_ obama_creates_more_czars_than_the_romanovs>; Barbara L. Schwemle et al., *The Debate Over Selected Presidential Assistants and Advisors: Appointment, Accountability, and Congressional Oversight*, R40856 (Washington, DC: Congressional Research Service, October 9, 2009).

[3] James R. Locher III, "Empowering Interagency Teams," *World Politics Review*, November 19, 2009. We also express our appreciation to Mr. Locher for his recommendations on improvements to an earlier draft of the paper.

[4] Christopher J. Lamb, "Redesigning White House Structures and Interagency Structures," in *Civilian Surge: Key to Complex Operations*, ed. Hans Binnendijk and Patrick M. Cronin (Washington, DC: NDU Press, 2009).

[5] John Podesta, cited in Schwemle et al.

[6] Project on National Security Reform (PNSR) and Center for the Study of the Presidency, *Forging a New Shield* (Arlington, VA: PNSR, 2008), available at <www.pnsr.org/data/files/pnsr_ forging_a_new_shield_report.pdf>. See preface, 34–35, 81, 140ff.

[7] The United States Commission on National Security/21st Century, Gary Hart and Warren Rudman, co-chairmen, *Seeking a National Strategy: A Concert For Preserving Security and Promoting Freedom*, Phase II Report on a U.S. National Security Strategy for the 21st Century (Washington, DC: U.S. Government Printing Office [GPO], April 15, 2000), 14.

[8] The Commission on the Intelligence Capabilities of the United States Regarding Weapons of Mass Destruction, Laurence H. Silberman and Charles S. Robb, co-chairmen, *Report to the President of the United States* (Washington, DC: GPO, March 31, 2005), 18, available at <www.gpoaccess.gov/wmd/ pdf/full_wmd_report.pdf>.

[9] See *Forging a New Shield*; and Morton H. Halperin, Priscilla Clapp, and Arnold Kanter, *Bureaucratic Politics and Foreign Policy* (Washington, DC: The Brookings Institution Press, 2006).

[10] *Forging a New Shield* catalogues many such critiques, but for more recent pithy senior assessments of the system by Obama administration officials, see Jim Garamone, "Flournoy Calls for Better Interagency Cooperation," American Forces Press Service, June 11, 2010, available at <www.defense. gov/news/newsarticle.aspx?id=59601>; and "Remarks as Delivered by Secretary of Defense Robert M. Gates," The Nixon Center, Washington, DC, February 24, 2010, available at <www.nixoncenter.org/in-dex.cfm?action=showpage&page=2009-Robert-Gates-Transcript>.

[11] A survey of over 250 books, articles, and studies on interagency cooperation in the U.S. Government found only one report that concluded that interagency cooperation is successful. See Christopher J. Lamb et al., "National Security Reform and the Security Environment," in *Global Strategic Assessment 2009: America's Security Role in a Changing World*, ed. Patrick M. Cronin (Washington, DC: NDU Press, 2009), 412–413.

[12] These levels of cross-organizational combined effort are advanced by Cathryn Downes (publication forthcoming), an expert on collaboration in the Information Resources Management College at National Defense University. For a complementary take on the topic, see Joyce Czajkowski, "Leading Successful Interinstitutional Collaborations Using the Collaboration Success Measurement Model," available at <www.chairacademy.com/conference/2007/papers/leading_successful_interinstitutional_collaborations.pdf>.

[13] James Q. Wilson, *Bureaucracy: What Government Agencies Do and Why They Do It* (New York: Basic Books, 1989).

[14] Tuan Samahon, "Potential Appointments Clause Issues Associated with Certain Types of 'Czars,'" Statement to the Committee on the Judiciary, U.S. Senate, October 6, 2009, available at <http://judiciary.senate.gov/pdf/10-06-09%20Samahon%20testimony.pdf>.

[15] John C. Harrison "Legal Issues Associated with Executive Branch 'Czars,'" Statement to the Committee on the Judiciary, Subcommittee on the Constitution, U.S. Senate, October 6, 2009, available at <http://judiciary.senate.gov/pdf/10-06-09%20Harrison%20testimony.pdf>.

[16] *Forging a New Shield*, 140.

[17] David Miller, "Hardly a Czar," May 16 2007, available at <www.cbsnews.com/stories/2007/05/16/opinion/main2812866.shtml>.

[18] Quotation from Joint Center for Operational Analysis staff interview of Ambassador Ryan Crocker, December 8, 2009.

[19] In the current administration, Lute's authority is further diminished since he has no direct access to the President but reports instead through the National Security Advisor. See Helene Cooper, "War Czar for Bush to Keep His Job," *The New York Times*, January 13, 2009, available at <http://thecaucus.blogs.nytimes.com/2009/01/13/war-czar-for-bush-to-keep-his-job/>.

[20] Arnold M. Howitt and Robyn L. Pangi, *Countering Terrorism: Dimensions of Preparedness* (Boston: The MIT Press, 2003), 25.

[21] "Secretary Clinton with Vice President Joe Biden Announce Appointment of Special Envoy for Middle East Peace George Mitchell and Special Representative for Afghanistan and Pakistan Richard Holbrooke," January 22, 2009, available at <www.state.gov/secretary/rm/2009a/01/115297.htm>.

[22] "Special Representative Holbrooke's Role in Afghanistan and Pakistan," February 6, 2009, available at <www.state.gov/secretary/rm/2009a/02/116314.htm>.

[23] National Security Directive 44, December 7, 2005, available at <www.fas.org/irp/offdocs/nspd/nspd-44.html>.

[24] Reconstruction and Stabilization Civilian Management Act of 2008, Section 1604, available at <http://frwebgate.access.gpo.gov/cgi-bin/getdoc.cgi?dbname=110_cong_public_laws&docid=f:publ417.110>.

[25] Rand Beers, "Structure Challenges Seminar," First panel, Proceedings from a PNSR Conference on Integrating Instruments of National Power in the New Security Environment, Washington, DC, July 25–26, 2007.

[26] "Joint Interagency Coordination Group (JIACG) Fact Sheet," available at <http://smallwarsjournal.com/documents/jiacgfactsheet.pdf>.

[27] Thomas P. Galvin, "Extending the Phase Zero Campaign Mindset: Ensuring Unity of Effort,"

Joint Force Quarterly 45 (2ᵈ Quarter, 2007), 49; Matthew F. Bogdanos, "Joint Interagency Cooperation: The First Step," *Joint Force Quarterly* 37 (2ᵈ Quarter, 2005), 17.

²⁸ U.S. House of Representatives, Committee on the Armed Services, Subcommittee on Oversight and Investigations, "Agency Stovepipes vs. Strategic Agility: Lessons We Need to Learn from Provincial Reconstruction Teams in Iraq and Afghanistan," April 2008, 42, available at <http://armed-services.house.gov/pdfs/Reports/PRT_Report.pdf>.

²⁹ Nima Abbaszadeh et al., *Provincial Reconstruction Teams: Lessons and Recommendations* (Princeton, NJ: The Woodrow Wilson School of International Affairs, January 2008), available at <http://wws.princeton.edu/research/pwreports_f07/wws591b.pdf>.

³⁰ U.S. Government Accountability Office (GAO), *Actions Needed to Address Stakeholder Concerns, Improve Interagency Collaboration, and Determine Full Costs Associated with U.S. Africa Command*, Report to Subcommittee on National Security and Foreign Affairs, Committee on Oversight and Government Reform, House of Representatives, GA–09–181 (Washington, DC: GAO, February 2009); House Committee on Oversight and Government Reform, "AFRICOM's Rationales, Roles and Progress on the Eve of Operations," July 15, 2008, available at <www.africom.mil/getArticle. asp?art=1921&lang=>; Richard Nelson, Director of the Center for Strategic and International Studies Homeland Security and Counterterrorism Program, "Powell Testifies before the Senate Homeland Security Committee on the Underwear Bomber," available at <www.rooseveltroom.net/powell-testifies-before-the-senate-homeland-security-committee-on-the-underwear-bomber/>; PNSR, *Toward Integrating Complex National Missions: Lessons from the National Counterterrorism Center's Directorate of Strategic Operational Planning* (Washington, DC: PNSR, February 2010), 11–19, available at <www.pnsr.org/data/files/pnsr_nctc_dsop_report.pdf>.

³¹ Shona L. Brown and Kathleen M. Eisenhardt, *Competing on the Edge: Strategy as Structured Chaos* (Boston: Harvard Business School, 1998).

³² Peter W. Rodman, *Presidential Command: Power, Leadership, and the Making of Foreign Policy from Richard Nixon to George W. Bush* (New York: Knopf, 2009), 277–278.

³³ Joseph J. Collins, *Choosing War: The Decision to Invade Iraq and Its Aftermath*, Institute for National Strategic Studies Occasional Paper 5 (Washington, DC: NDU Press, 2008).

³⁴ The official title of the position is "Coordinator for the Prevention of Weapons of Mass Destruction Proliferation and Terrorism."

³⁵ Public Law 110–53, "Implementing Recommendations of the 9/11 Commission Act of 2007," 110ᵗʰ Cong., 1ˢᵗ sess., August 3, 2007.

³⁶ Section 102A(f)(1)(A)(ii) of the National Security Act of 1947 (50 U.S.C. 403–1[f][1][A][ii]).

³⁷ Public Law 108–458, Intelligence Reform and Terrorism Prevention Act of 2004, Section 102A, December 17, 2004, available at <www.nctc.gov/docs/pl108_458.pdf>.

³⁸ Public Law 108–458, Section 1018. Emphasis added.

³⁹ The title of the program initially was "Civil Operations and *Revolutionary* Development Support," but was changed in 1970.

⁴⁰ National Security Action Memorandum No. 362: Responsibility for U.S. Role in Pacification (Revolutionary Development), May 9, 1967, available at <www.lbjlib.utexas.edu/johnson/archives.hom/NSAMs/nsam362.asp>.

[41] Executive Order 12880, National Drug Control Program, November 16 1993, available at <http://nodis3.gsfc.nasa.gov/displayEO.cfm?id=EO_12880_>.

[42] For an approach favoring an interagency architect whose influence would depend on budgetary authority, see Ashton B. Carter, "The Architecture of Government in the Face of Terrorism," *International Security* 26, no. 3 (Winter 2001/2002), 5–23.

[43] GAO, "Drug Control: ONDCP Efforts to Manage the National Drug Control Budget," May 14, 1999, available at <www.gao.gov/archive/1999/gg99080.pdf>.

[44] John D. Jernegan, "The Ambassador and the Country Team," July 1963, cited in Barry K. Simmons, "Executing U.S. Foreign Policy Through the Country Team Concept," *The Air Force Law Review* 37 (1994).

[45] "Letter from the Deputy Under Secretary of State for Administration (Crockett) to the Ambassador to Germany (McGhee)," *Foreign Relations of the United States, 1964–1968*, vol. XXXIII, *Organization and Management of Foreign Policy*; United Nations, Document 28.

[46] Barry K. Simmons, "Executing U.S. Foreign Policy Through the Country Team Concept," *The Air Force Law Review* 37 (1994).

[47] Ibid.

[48] "Circular Telegram from the Department of State to All Diplomatic Missions," *Foreign Relations of the United States, 1955–1957*, vol. X, *Foreign Aid and Economic Defense Policy*, Document 21 (Washington, DC: GPO, July 24, 1956), available at <http://history.state.gov/historicaldocuments/frus1955-57v10/d21>.

[49] *Ambassador Extraordinary and Plenipotentiary* is the internationally recognized title for the personal representative of the head of state, and, internationally, the head of state is presumed to speak for all of the state he/she heads. Also known as *Chief of Mission*, this American bureaucratic usage refers to the responsibility for the management of all internal operations. Although an Ambassador is a State Department employee for administrative purposes and is required to report through the Secretary of State, he/she is the President's personal representative during his/her posting and, in therefore in a narrow sense, not a Department of State representative.

[50] "Memorandum from the Under Secretary of State (Bowles) to All Chiefs of Mission," *Foreign Relations of the United States, 1961–1963*, vol. XXV, *Organizations of Foreign Policy* (Washington, DC: GPO, July 8, 1961).

[51] "Memorandum from the Deputy Under Secretary of State for Administration (Crockett) to the President's Special Assistant (Busby)," *Foreign Relations of the United States, 1964–1968*, vol. XXXIII, *Organization and Management of Foreign Policy* (Washington, DC: GPO, January 25, 1965).

[52] 22 U.S.C. 3927, Title 22, Chapter 52, Subchapter II, Section 3927. We are indebted to Richard Best, Congressional Research Service, a member of PNSR's structure working groups, for this observation.

[53] The authors are indebted to Ambassador Thomas Krajeski for these points.

[54] National Security Decision Directive 38, June 2, 1982, available at <www.state.gov/m/pri/nsdd/>.

[55] We are indebted to Ambassador Richard Norland for this point.

[56] Congress and the President share the authority for creating executive branch organization.

See Cody Brown and Jeffrey Ratner, "White House Czars: Is Congress to Blame?" *Christian Science Monitor*, October 19, 2009. The authors were legal staff working for the Project on National Security Reform. Brown noted in followup personal correspondence about the article that Congress' authority over the organization of the executive branch dates to the establishment of the three departments in 1789, but that the President has his own authority over foreign affairs, which he has exercised to establish organizations.

[57] *Foreign Relations of the United States, 1969–1976*, vol. II, *Organization and Management of U.S. Foreign Policy, 1969–1972*, Document 311 (Washington, DC: GPO, n.d.).

[58] For a notorious case of Ambassador–combatant commander conflict that escalated to the top echelons of the national security establishment, see David LaGesse, "U.S. officials clash over control of troops in Latin America State Department," *The Dallas Morning News*, June 15, 1994.

[59] Charles Ray, "Defining Lines of Authority," *Armed Forces Journal International*, February 2009.

[60] Shawn Zeller, "Who's in Charge Here?" *Foreign Service Journal*, December 2007.

[61] Special Inspector General for Iraq Reconstruction (SIGIR), *Hard Lessons: The Iraq Reconstruction Experience* (Washington, DC: GPO, 2009), 341, available at <www.sigir.mil/files/HardLessons/Hard_Lessons_Report.pdf>.

[62] Robert B. Oakley and Michael J. Casey, *The Country Team: Restructuring America's First Line of Engagement,* INSS Strategic Forum 227 (Washington, DC: NDU Press, 2007).

[63] Some assert the Country Team works better in crises and others that it is overwhelmed during crises as organizations fallback on their cultural norms. See respectively, Simmons; and David C. Litt, "Transforming America's collaborative crisis response capability: The executive education dimension," *American Diplomacy*, July 21, 2009.

[64] Edward Peck, "Chief-of-Mission Authority: A Powerful but Underused Tool," *Foreign Service Journal*, December 2007.

[65] For an approach favoring an interagency architect whose influence would depend on budgetary authority, see Carter.

[66] We are indebted to Cody Brown, formerly Chief of Legal Research at PNSR, for this preliminary analysis.

[67] For a good review of this issue, see Gordon Lederman, "National Security Reform for the Twenty-first Century: A New National Security Act and Reflections on Legislation's Role in Organizational Change," *Journal of National Security Law and Policy*, vol. 3 (2009), 363ff.

[68] Ibid.

[69] Executive Order 13456, "Further Amendment of Executive Order 11858 Concerning Foreign Investment in the United States," January 23, 2008, available at <www.fas.org/irp/offdocs/eo/eo-13456.html>.

[70] See "JIATF–South: The Best Known, Least Understood Interagency Success," forthcoming from NDU Press.

[71] *Forging a New Shield*, 526.

[72] Edward Marks, "The Next Generation Department of State," *Foreign Service Journal*, May 2010.

[73] Quotation from Joint Center for Operational Analysis staff interview of Ambassador Ryan Crocker, December 8, 2009.

[74] John H. Pendleton, Director of Defense Capabilities and Management, "National Security: Interagency Collaboration Practices and Challenges at DOD's Southern and Africa Commands," Testimony before the Subcommittee on National Security and Foreign Affairs, Committee on Oversight and Government Reform, House of Representatives, July 28, 2010, available at <www.gao.gov/new.items/d10962t.pdf>.

[75] We are indebted to Bernard T. Carreau for this point in an earlier review of the paper. The same point is made by many national security reviews. See the legislative reform package recommended in *The QDR in Perspective: Meeting America's National Security Needs in the 21st Century*, The Final Report of the Quadrennial Defense Review Independent Panel, Stephen J. Hadley and William J. Perry, co-chairmen (Washington, DC: U.S. Institute of Peace, 2010), available at <www.usip.org/files/qdr/qdrreport.pdf>.

[76] We are indebted to James Locher for this historical note.

[77] See Christopher J. Lamb and Martin Cinnamond, *Unity of Effort: Key to Success in Afghanistan*, INSS Strategic Forum 248 (Washington, DC: NDU Press, October 2009).

[78] Simmons quotes a senior national security official asserting decades ago that interagency coordination at the operational and tactical levels is "one of the most neglected aspects of the national security process, yet it is one whose importance can hardly be overestimated." Innumerable similar references could be cited. See Simmons, 135.

[79] Stephen J. Hadley and William J. Perry, co-chairmen, "The QDR in Perspective: Meeting America's National Security Needs in the 21st Century," The Final Report of the Quadrennial Defense Review Independent Panel.

[80] GAO, *Interagency Collaboration: Key Issues for Congressional Oversight of National Security Strategies, Organizations, Workforce, and Information Sharing*, GAO-09-904SP (Washington, DC: GAO, September 2009), available at <www.gao.gov/new.items/d09904sp.pdf>.

[81] SIGIR, 333. We express our appreciation to Ms. Ginger M. Cruz, Deputy Inspector General, Office of the Special Inspector General for Iraq Reconstruction, for her insights on improvements to an earlier draft of the paper.

[82] Ibid., 30.

[83] It would probably be easiest to exercise the new authority and approach following a new administration or a changeover in Cabinet officials so that the President could clarify his expectations to the new department heads.

Acknowledgments

The authors wish to express appreciation to those who took time from their busy schedules to comment on earlier drafts of this monograph, particularly James R. Locher III, Ambassador Thomas Krajeski, Ambassador Richard Norland, and Ms. Ginger M. Cruz. We also want to recognize the excellent early research assistance from Evan Munsing on portions of the paper identifying inadequate existing authorities in existing interagency constructs.

About the Authors

Dr. Christopher J. Lamb serves as the Director of the Center for Strategic Research in the Institute for National Strategic Studies (INSS) at the National Defense University (NDU), and is a Distinguished Research Fellow. He conducts research on national security strategy, policy and organizational reform, and on defense strategy, requirements, plans, and programs. In 2008, Dr. Lamb was assigned to lead the Project for National Security Reform study of the national security system, which led to the 2008 report, *Forging a New Shield.* Prior to joining INSS in 2004, Dr. Lamb served as the Deputy Assistant Secretary of Defense for Resources and Plans where he had oversight of war plans, requirements, acquisition, and resource allocation matters for the Under Secretary of Defense (Policy). Previously, he served as Deputy Director for Military Development on the State Department's Interagency Task Force for Military Stabilization in the Balkans; as Director of Policy Planning in the Office of the Assistant Secretary of Defense for Special Operations and Low-Intensity Conflict; and from 1985 to 1992 as a Foreign Service Officer in Haiti and Ivory Coast. He received his doctorate in International Relations from Georgetown University in 1986. Dr. Lamb has received the Chairman of the Joint Chiefs of Staff Joint Distinguished Civilian Service Award, the Presidential Rank Award for Meritorious Senior Executive Service, the Superior Honor award from the Department of State, and Meritorious Civilian Service awards from the Department of Defense.

Ambassador (Ret.) Edward Marks is a retired Senior Foreign Service Officer with a 40-year career involving service in nine countries, the United Nations (UN) in New York, and Washington, DC. Senior positions included Deputy Coordinator for Counter-Terrorism in the Department of State, 1982–1985, Ambassador to Guinea-Bissau and Cape Verde, and Deputy U.S. Representative to the Economic and Social Council of the UN. He was recalled to active duty in 2002 to serve as the first Department of State representative in the Joint Inter-Agency Coordination Group on Counterterrorism at U.S. Pacific Command. A graduate of the National War College, Ambassador Marks was a Distinguished Visiting Fellow in the Center for Strategic and International Studies, Visiting Senior Fellow in INSS at NDU, and is currently a Distinguished Senior Fellow at George Mason University and a Founding Trustee of the Command and General Staff College Foundation. He is a graduate of the University of Michigan (BA) and the University of Oklahoma (MA). Ambassador Marks was actively engaged in the Project on National Security Reform, out of which came his work on "The Next Generation Department of State."